Original title:
Under the Pine's Shadow

Copyright © 2025 Creative Arts Management OÜ
All rights reserved.

Author: Clara Whitfield
ISBN HARDBACK: 978-1-80567-184-8
ISBN PAPERBACK: 978-1-80567-483-2

The Realm of Green Embrace

In a land where squirrels play,
And giggling leaves sway all day.
Trees wear hats of mossy green,
A comedian's stage, a woodland scene.

Beneath branches, we all conspire,
To tell tales that never tire.
Acorns drop like laughter's sound,
In this realm, joy's always found.

Hidden Paths of Solitary Ramblings

On paths where shadows play hide and seek,
I talk to flowers; they never speak.
Rabbits chuckle, running in haste,
To dodge my ponderings, none to waste.

A gnome whispers secrets to the breeze,
While ants march on like tiny armies.
I trip over roots that seem alive,
Nature's pranks make my spirits thrive!

Shadows Dancing in the Breeze

Shadows pirouette, a silent jest,
As the sun peeks out for a little rest.
A grasshopper jumps like it's all a show,
While twirling leaves join in the flow.

Echoes of laughter skirt through the air,
As whimsical whispers scatter with flair.
I chase the sunbeams, joyfully absurd,
In a chat with a crow, I've hardly heard!

Where the World Softly Pauses

Where the world takes a funny break,
And even the streams seem to shake.
Clouds tickle the mountains, oh what a sight,
As the wind shares jokes, day turns to night.

Crickets serenade a night full of glee,
While owls roll their eyes, 'Just let it be.'
Hiccups of stars burst in the sky,
In this pause, I laugh at the by and by.

Nature's Chosen Sanctuary

In a cozy nook where squirrels play,
The raccoons laugh at the end of the day.
A frog leaps high, but slips on a log,
While the owl hoots, thinking it's a dog.

A family of ants, with snacks to share,
March in a line, without a care.
The winds tease leaves, as if to say,
"Don't get too comfy, you'll blow away!"

A turtle sunbathes, a comical sight,
While a chubby chipmunk scurries with fright.
The earthworms giggle, all snug in their mud,
Debating who's fatter — who's who, is the bud!

With jokes in the breeze and laughter in trees,
The creatures rejoice, doing just as they please.
In this silly realm where nature takes charge,
Every wacky moment feels wonderfully large.

Songs of the Wind and Trees

The trees whisper secrets, a humorous plot,
As the beetles groove in a dance so hot.
A rabbit hops in, with ears in a flap,
As the squirrels chuckle, planning a nap.

The breeze brings a tickle, a feathered delight,
As the birds crack jokes from morning till night.
A twig snaps suddenly, what a loud launch!
Everyone jumps, as they think there's a brunch!

A wise old raccoon offers sage advice,
"Don't be too lazy, or you'll roll the dice."
Yet up in the boughs, a sloth takes his time,
Gazing at clouds as if they'd rhyme.

So join in the chorus, let laughter abound,
In the woods where joy is forever found.
With each rustling leaf and each playful breeze,
Life's a comedy penned by the trees.

Where the Needles Fall

Squirrels plotting heists with glee,
Nuts and acorns stored for free.
A dance of shadows, cheeky and bold,
While I sip lemonade, feeling quite old.

The branches stretch, like arms to play,
Tickling the clouds at close of day.
A branch breaks loose, don't drop that cup!
That ice-cold drink? Oh, fill it up!

Solace in the Dense Foliage

In a grove where laughter spills,
Frogs wear crowns, oh what a thrill!
Beneath the leaves, a chorus of croaks,
Ribbiting songs from silly folks.

A raccoon winks, with mischief in eyes,
While birds gossip about new skies.
The breeze brings whispers, tickles the ear,
What's that? A pine cone? Oh dear, oh dear!

The Quietude of Twilight Woods

As dusk creeps in, the critters rave,
Beneath the boughs, they start to behave.
A fox dons a scarf, all dapper and neat,
While owls hold court, and rabbits tweet.

A firefly army lights up the dance,
While I trip over roots in a fanciful prance.
Oh twilight glow, what a sight you make,
Just watch for the branch - it's a real heartache!

Beneath the Whispering Woodlands

Trees gossiping secrets, they don't even care,
While chipmunks play poker, with quite the flair.
I join their game, but lose every round,
Those furry creatures sure know how to astound.

With whispers of pine and laughter so bright,
The sun sets low, surrendering light.
I tip my hat to the wise old bird,
"Wish me luck next time," was all that I heard!

Nature's Softest Rustle

In the woods where squirrels play,
They chatter gossip, night and day.
A leaf falls down, a gentle thud,
It's just the trees letting out a dud.

The rabbits hop, a funny sight,
Dressed in coats that are just too tight.
A chipmunk dreams of acorn stew,
While ants march by, as if they knew.

A breeze tickles all who stand,
As nature giggles at our hand.
The mushrooms laugh at toadstool pies,
And shadows dance beneath the skies.

So come, let's stomp and shake a leg,
The forest's fun is quite the peg.
With rustle, chuckles fill the air,
Nature's soft laughter everywhere.

The Kingdom of Swaying Sentinels

Tall trees stand in regal rows,
With branches swaying, no one knows.
They wave hello with a leafy cheer,
And gossip winds that tickle the ear.

A squirrel wears a dapper hat,
To strut around and chat with that.
The bees concoct sweet melodies,
As flowers smile and sway with ease.

A raccoon with a sly, wide grin,
Tries to steal from bin to bin.
But all around, the owls just hoot,
That this is not a bedtime snoot.

So if you wander through this land,
Expect the trees to take your hand.
In this kingdom where laughter's rife,
The whispers bring all things to life.

A Conversation with Tall Spirits

A breeze tickles the bark and gum,
While trees lean close, and gently hum.
"I saw a bird!," one tree did say,
"It stole my hat, then flew away!"

A crow just caws, with sass and style,
"Those silly hats make me smile!"
The trunks exchange their funny tales,
While rustling leaves sway like sails.

"Do you think the sun is hot today?"
Asks a tree with branches in dismay.
"Not half as hot as my cousin's roots,"
One answers back, "He sports green boots!"

Laughter rings through boughs and woods,
As they band together, sharing goods.
For trees that talk have much to say,
In this forest where chuckles play.

Traces of Silence in Green Light

In hush of green where shadows dwell,
The ferns could tell a cheerful spell.
A snail prances in a racing suit,
While whispering flowers share the loot.

Swaying fronds play hide and seek,
"Come find me quick!" they squeak and peek.
Crickets chirp like a buzzing band,
As nature's laughter fills the land.

The sunbeams dance on dew-kissed grass,
While critters sit and watch the class.
A ant parade with tiny hats,
To show the world just how they chat.

So when you tread on paths of light,
Remember fun is never slight.
In silence wrapped like gifts so bright,
Lies joy and giggles, pure delight.

The Stillness of Time's Guardians

Amidst the branches, squirrels prance,
They've got a dance, a nutty romance.
Beneath the watch of ancient trees,
Even time chuckles in the breeze.

A wise old owl winks in the night,
While rabbits frolic in sheer delight.
The forest's whispers, such a delight,
Crickets chirp jokes till morning light.

Mice in tuxedos, they sip their tea,
Charming the bugs with such glee.
Each shadow laughs, a giggling spree,
Guardians of time, quite the sight to see.

Moose try yoga, strike a pose,
Bending and stretching, lord knows!
With each playful blunder they make,
The calm stillness, it starts to break.

Beneath the Needle-Laden Sky

Beneath sharp needles, critters plot,
A prank by raccoons, oh what a lot!
They tiptoe round with mischief in mind,
Creating chaos, of every kind.

A porcupine with a flair for fashion,
Wears a crown of thorns, oh the passion!
He struts and prances, a regal show,
While the chipmunks cheer, 'You steal the show!'

The shadows stretch and twist with glee,
As shadows meet for yoga, yes indeed!
A game of tag, where acorns fly,
Giggles echo, nearly reach the sky.

In this woodland mix-up, full of fun,
Every day feels like a wild run.
So let's toast to trees, making us smile,
With each new caper, we roam in style.

Tales of the Coniferous Heart

In the woods where mischief dwells,
Squirrels tell tales, oh do they yell!
Each story spins a catchy tune,
As night drapes over, beneath the moon.

Pinecones falling like little bombs,
Gathering groups of woodland chums.
"Oh dear," says the badger, "don't be shy,"
"Collect them all! We'll throw and fly!"

A turtle gossip, slow and wise,
Spills the beans amidst the sighs.
"Did you hear about that tree so spry?"
"It dances nightly! Oh me, oh my!"

With laughter echoing through each branch,
Every creature gives the world a chance.
In this tall haven, joy's the art,
We weave our stories, to the heart.

Overture in the Woodland

The trees are drummers, tapping along,
As branches sway, they hum a song.
With acorns falling like jealous notes,
The woodland critters dance in coats.

A snake in spectacles reads the news,
Woodpeckers laugh, sharing their views.
"Did the owl hear that joke about time?"
"She snores, she snores, oh what a rhyme!"

A hedgehog dreams of fame and glory,
Plans to write his forest story.
While turtles challenge them to a race,
The slowest one, still wins with grace.

As the sun dips low, colors ignite,
A symphony plays, all feeling bright.
In the grand overture of leafy cheer,
Forest fun replays, year after year.

Beneath the Watchful Green Eyes

The squirrels plot a heist today,
A stash of nuts they'll gleefully play.
With tiny paws and antics so spry,
They gather treasures, oh my, oh my!

A chubby raccoon lurks close in the brush,
Eating stolen snacks in a magical hush.
He tips his hat, shimmies with glee,
'These woodland snacks are meant for me!'

The wise old owl hoots loud and clear,
'Stop those bandits, oh dear, oh dear!'
But all he does is roll his big eyes,
As the critters burst forth in silly disguise.

Now the breeze carries laughter and cheer,
As mischief unfolds in this leafy sphere.
With giggles echoing through the high trees,
Life here is fun, as wild as a tease!

The Pulse of the Woodland Heart

A bunny hops side to side,
Chasing shadows, he cannot hide.
His floppy ears are quite the sight,
As he zooms past, a comical fright!

Nearby, a turtle slowly grins,
Saying, 'Catch me if you can, my friends!'
But he deserves a round of applause,
For moving with such fancy cause!

A dance-off starts near an old oak tree,
With crickets chirping a melody.
The creatures twirl, stomp, and sway,
In this giggle-fest of a perfect day.

The woodland heart beats loud with fun,
As sunbeams shimmer, one by one.
In laughter's light, they all partake,
A joy that's real, not just a fake!

Songs Sung by Breeze and Pine

The wind whistles tunes through branches high,
While ants march in sync, oh my, oh my!
They sing of adventures and tasty crumbs,
While dancing daintily, oh, how it hums!

A family of deer joins in the ruse,
With bounding steps in their shiny shoes.
They prance and leap, a delightful sight,
In sync with the rhythm, from morning till night.

The chipmunks chime in with quick little tricks,
Juggling acorns with zany flicks.
With each little tumble, the laughter rings,
As the forest joins in, and everyone sings.

Together they weave a tapestry bright,
Of merry moments that feel just right.
With nature's song filling the air,
They dance through life without a care!

Journey into the Emerald Oasis

Through the bushes, a parade begins,
With frogs in tuxedos, oh where to begin?
They hop and croak, a fancy display,
As the sun peeks in to join the ballet!

A lizard does somersaults on the ground,
While butterflies flutter and twirl all around.
They're training for contests, they have no shame,
In their playful world, it's all just a game.

The flowers giggle in colorful rows,
As the breeze tells tales that nobody knows.
The mushrooms dance with curious flair,
As they join the fun in the fresh woodland air.

Together they journey, a lively parade,
Creating laughter as friendships are made.
In this emerald realm where whimsy unfolds,
All join the adventure; a sight to behold!

Nestled in the Embrace of Branches

A squirrel stole my sandwich, I swear,
He wore a tiny hat, that little dare.
He danced and twirled, oh what a sight,
As I laughed and chased him in delight.

The sun peeked through, a tickling tease,
While ants marched in line, quite the expertise.
I tripped on roots, a comical fall,
The nature committee held its call.

Birds chirped gossip, loud and clear,
About the acorn heist, let's give a cheer!
The wind made wishes, swayed our hair,
Nature's comedy, a joyful affair.

So, gather your giggles, draw near my friends,
In this green theater, laughter never ends.
With critters aplenty and trees so grand,
We find our joy in this wacky land.

Shadows of the Ancient Sentinels

The trees gossip in shades, can you hear?
They trade juicy tales of the foxes that leer.
A raccoon in a mask, a midnight bandit,
Swiped my snacks, oh, he really planned it!

A nearby owl, wise and drowsy,
Snores so loud, it's almost rousy.
"Get off my lawn!" he hoots from the fray,
To the squirrels who frolic and play all day.

The shadows flicker, hold secrets tight,
Like a game of hide and seek in the night.
Branches swoop low, a ceiling of glee,
Nature's theatre, just wait and see!

In the forest's embrace, we laugh and jest,
With quirky characters, it's truly the best.
So come join the fun, don't be so shy,
Under the canopy, we'll reach for the sky!

Beneath the Boughs of Solitude

A tortoise strolled, slow as can be,
With a party hat on, just look and see!
He claimed he ran marathons at night,
While I just snickered, what a silly sight!

A deer pranced by, shaking its head,
Wearing flowers, its fashion widely spread.
"Fancy dinner?" it asked with a grin,
When all it wanted was some sweet grass to win.

The breeze told secrets, tickled my ears,
Of frogs at karaoke, singing their spheres.
Laughter echoed, a joyful croak,
As the trees bobbed along with each joke.

Here in this haven, life's a charade,
With critters galore, and a shade parade.
Let the whimsy of nature wrap you so tight,
In solitude's garden, everything's light!

The Tranquil Gaze of Nature

A butterfly flitted, mischief in tow,
It borrowed my hat, just for a show.
With a twirl and a flap, it took to the sky,
Leaving me chuckling as it waved goodbye.

Grasshoppers leaped, rehearsing their dance,
Claiming it's Broadway, giving dreams a chance.
Who needed a stage when you had mere grass?
Critters combine for a moment to sass!

An ant formed a band, with sticks as guitars,
Belting out tunes under the stars.
"Life's all about rhythm!" the ladybug cried,
As those in the crowd cheered and sighed.

So, marvel my friends, at this woodland spree,
Where laughter and music reign wild and free.
In nature's embrace, let joy find its way,
With funny little moments brightening our day.

Beneath the Crown of Forked Branches

A squirrel tried to steal my lunch,
He thought he'd sneak, but I had a hunch.
With acorns piled high in his nest,
He planned to host a furry fest!

A bird then joined, with a cheeky squawk,
Declaring loudly, 'Let's take a walk!'
They both wore hats made out of leaves,
Crowning themselves, like forest thieves.

The sun peeked through in a wink,
As raccoons danced, all in sync.
A wild parade of nature's crew,
In the grand circus of the dew.

Laughter echoed from twig to tree,
As every creature yelled, "Come see!"
Beneath this crown of branches wide,
Fun's the secret, there's no need to hide.

The Language of the Forest

The trees gossip in their leafy tones,
About the squirrels and their broken phones.
'Look at them,' one willow said with glee,
'Chasing their tails as if they're carefree!'

Mice giggled at a stuttering crow,
Who tripped over roots, putting on a show.
They said, 'Is it true he's got no sense?'
And roared with laughter, fully convinced!

Underneath, where shadows lie,
Ants held debates as the firefly.
They'd argue about crumbs and a lost snack,
In this vibrant world, there's no lack.

Whispers of joy from the leaves' embrace,
In the forest's language, a funny place.
Where every critter has a story to tell,
Of mischief and giggles, all under the spell!

Glimpses of Serenity

A frog in a pond wore a tiny hat,
Said, 'I'm the king, how about that?'
With every leap, he took a bow,
The water rippling, 'You're silly now!'

A turtle too slow, with a grin so wide,
Challenged the breeze to come for a ride.
While fish raced by, swift as a dream,
Laughing aloud, 'We're part of the theme!'

In corners of peace, where daisies sway,
A ladybug danced, enjoying the day.
With stripes of delight on her tiny back,
Shimming through petals, all in a whack.

Glimpses of joy in this rhythm of calm,
A playful tune, like a soothing balm.
Nature's party, wild and free,
Serenity echoes, come join, you'll see!

Swaying Silhouettes of Peace

A cat sprawled out, a king in the sun,
Dreaming of fish and a day full of fun.
He stretched with a yawn, then rolled on his back,
While a woodpecker drummed, 'Check the snack!'

Bunnies wiggled, all quiet and shy,
They wondered if clouds could dance in the sky.
'They float too well,' one muttered with cheer,
'But we can hop higher, that's our frontier!'

Overhead, the butterflies flew,
Playing tag with the wind, as they drew.
The shadows wiggled like worms in a jig,
As nature chuckled, feeling quite big.

In swaying shapes, where joy meets release,
The laughter of creatures, a vivid feast.
So take a moment, let worries cease,
In these playful silhouettes, find your peace.

Reflections in Verdant Hues

Amidst the leaves, a squirrel pranced,
Chasing its tail as if it danced.
A bumblebee buzzed with a sunny cheer,
Waved at a flower that looked quite dear.

The grass tickled toes in playful delight,
While frogs croaked jokes, with great insight.
A chipmunk snickered, hiding a nut,
While the owl judged with a wise old strut.

They feasted on laughter, no room for gloom,
As fireflies flickered, lighting the room.
With every chuckle, the forest did sway,
To the funny tunes of a bright summer day.

Nature's comedy, a wondrous play,
Where even the silence could giggle away.
In hues of green, life's laughter sings,
A tapestry woven of whimsical things.

Beneath the Tall Sentinels

A rabbit wore glasses and read a good book,
While a turtle ran, oh what a hook!
They raced past shadows, in squeaky delight,
As birds dropped jokes that took flight.

The wind whispered secrets, all in good fun,
While ants played hide-and-seek in the sun.
An acorn dropped, and a giggle was shared,
As everyone thought, 'Who's really prepared?'

A bear with a bow tied absurdly neat,
Juggled ripe berries, what a silly feat!
He stumbled and tumbled, oh what a sight,
As critters all laughed, it felt so right.

The tall trees swayed, joining in the jest,
With leaves clapping hands, feeling quite blessed.
In this enchanting grove, joy's the decree,
Where laughter is plenty, and time feels free.

Echoes of the Forest Floor

On the forest floor, a dance did commence,
With mushrooms as partners, it made no sense!
A hedgehog in socks twirled with great flair,
While beetles rolled dice without a care.

The breeze played a tune that was squawky and bright,
Even the rocks seemed to wobble with light.
A snail spun around, in a sequined shell,
Claiming that style mattered very well.

The rabbits threw carrots like confetti high,
While squirrels debated on who could fly.
An owl stopped by, more curious than wise,
To see the strange antics and wild, happy cries.

In a symphony of giggles, the woods felt alive,
As echoes of laughter made all creatures thrive.
With every rustle and chuckle so sweet,
The forest realized it was quite the treat.

Lullabies of Resin and Earth

A caterpillar crooned lullabies low,
As crickets tapped feet in a rhythmic flow.
The groundhogs chimed in with a chuckle or two,
While the bushes swayed, dancing like dew.

At twilight's embrace, the shadows did play,
Chasing the stars who were late on their way.
A raccoon with rhythm banged on a drum,
Calling all critters, 'Come join, have fun!'

The fireflies glowed like disco lights,
As laughter erupted from the hungry bites.
A fox told tall tales about pirate ships,
While frogs offered snacks in honest quips.

As the moonlight giggled, the night wore a grin,
In this cozy haven, all felt the spin.
With resinous dreams and playful mirth,
The forest sang softly, a lullaby of earth.

The Serenity of Nature's Retreat

In a cozy nook where the squirrels jest,
A woodpecker drums on a tree for a quest.
A rabbit hops by, wearing a hat,
Sipping on tea while chatting with a cat.

Leaves dance around like they're lost in the breeze,
A frog croaks a tune, intending to please.
The sun winks down, showing off its round grin,
While ants in a row march, looking for kin.

Nearby, a raccoon steals snacks from a box,
Painting the scene with some whimsical flocks.
All nature's creatures, so cozy and bright,
Invite passerby to stay and delight.

Here's to the laughter that nature will bring,
Where every small critter seems ready to sing.
In moments of joy, we're all set to play,
In this wild world, come join us today!

Ferns in the Gentle Shade

Ferns stretch their arms, waving hello,
As a chipmunk struts with a fashionable flow.
A tortoise ambles, boots laced tight,
With dreams of the race he'll win by twilight.

Sunbeams peek through with a cheeky tease,
As butterflies dance in the soft, warm breeze.
A snail takes a selfie, poses with flair,
While the hedgehog sighs, "I just need some air!"

The grass tickles toes, oh what a delight,
When a parrot squawks jokes, thinking he's bright.
Laughter unfolds under leafy embrace,
In this funny haven, there's always a space.

When evening rolls in, the jokes won't fall flat,
With memories made, here's where we sat.
Ferns keep the secrets; they'd laugh if they could,
In the gentle shade, life's always so good!

A Symphony of Needles and Sunlight

In the needle's hum, a quirky refrain,
As a hedgehog complains of his spiky terrain.
A raccoon with rhythm taps on a drum,
Joining the chorus—a wild, funny strum.

The sunlight beams down, casting shadows that wiggle,
A rabbit hops past, then leaps with a giggle.
An owl squints, unsure of the mood,
As fireflies flash their glow, oh so crude!

Each note in the glade makes the flowers sway,
While the frogs on a log start the musical play.
A turtle in shades says, "Give me a break,
I'm not part of this show; I'm just here for cake!"

As night falls, the symphony shifts to a hum,
Nature's orchestra, a collective thrum.
With laughter and joy, in this natural dome,
The needles, the critters, they all feel like home.

In the Quiet Glade of Time

In the quiet glade where the sunflowers grin,
A mole plays the piano—he's really quite thin.
A squirrel dashes by with a stash of old fries,
While a kitten observes with wide-open eyes.

Funny whispers echo 'neath branches that smile,
As crickets recite poems in their own style.
The breeze shakes a branch, sending leaves on a spree,
And a bumblebee buzzes, "Just listen to me!"

A ladybug jokes about fashion, she said,
"I don't need a dress, just a leaf for my head!"
And the fox in the clearing, sleek, fast, and spry,
Cannot help but chuckle as butterflies fly.

As dusk hugs the day with a soft, tender glow,
Nature's own chorus sings sweetly below.
In this whimsical space, time dances away,
Let laughter and joy be our guides as we play!

Shadows of Timeless Tranquility

In the woods where squirrels laugh,
A raccoon stole my snack last half.
He danced around without a care,
While I just stood, caught in despair.

Sunlight flickers, shadows play,
My hat's gone—who can say?
A chipmunk wears it, looking grand,
I sigh and watch, can't make a stand.

Lost my shoe to a slippery vine,
Tripped on roots, oh, isn't it divine?
Laughter echoes, fills the air,
Nature's got jokes—beyond compare.

Time moves slow, yet I'm stuck fast,
Can't help but grin, what a blast!
Undercover of green so lush,
Life's funny here—no need to rush.

Nestled in Nature's Arms

Beneath the branches, low and wide,
A toad jumped in, what a slide!
Splash of mud, a perfect art,
My picnic's toast, oh, that's smart!

The birds up high converse and chat,
What's so funny about that cat?
It creeps around with stealthy grace,
Then trips and lands right on its face!

The wind whispers tales, oh so sly,
Why did the beetle just fly by?
It changed direction in mid-air,
Looks like fun's afoot, beware!

Lying back, clouds float so free,
Imagining a world where I'd be—
A critter full of puns, no doubt,
Life's joys here, let's share a shout!

Beneath the Coniferous Veil

A squirrel launched his acorn high,
It missed its mark and—for a cry!
A soft thud followed by some rustling,
Thought I'd find treasure—just a tussling!

The shadows dance, a jig so sweet,
Beneath green boughs, mischiefs greet.
A bear in shades, how absurd it seems,
Like he's auditioning for my wildest dreams!

A mouse with glasses reads a book,
While bunnies giggle—oh, take a look!
They plan a heist of carrots bright,
With all their might, a comical sight!

Time drifts by, but laughter stays,
In nature's arms, we find our ways.
So linger here, let whims flow free,
Among the trees, just you and me.

Dreams Cradled by Pine

Whispers rustle in the dark,
A firefly glows like a spark.
My cozy blanket, snug and tight,
A raccoon thinks it's quite a sight!

The night is filled with shooing sounds,
Critters scatter all around.
An owl hoots a silly tune,
While crickets chirp a hearty croon.

Laughter bubbles under the stars,
In this wild, we're all the char stars!
A fox does cartwheels, what a sight,
While I just chuckle at his flight!

Pine-scented dreams, oh what fun,
This forest dance has just begun.
Let's tap our feet and sway with glee,
For laughter's here, wild and free!

Whispers Beneath the Canopy

Squirrels chatter, plotting a heist,
They steal my snack, oh how nice!
With little paws and crafty grins,
They scurry away, where mischief begins.

A bird serenades in a wobbly tune,
While I chuckle at the clumsy raccoon.
It tumbles down with a startled yelp,
And I can't help but laugh at its whelp.

Secrets of the Woodland Grove

The trees gossip about the ants,
Dancing wildly in their tiny pants.
They march in lines, a comical sight,
Two-stepping clumsily, oh what a fright!

Frogs take cover, in the mud they leap,
As nearby rabbits make a pile and heap.
They bounce around in springy delight,
I don't know whether to laugh or take flight!

Dappled Light on Forest Floor

Sunbeams play hide and seek on the ground,
As bugs gather, a buzzing sound.
They zoom and zip, like tiny drones,
Pretending to be kings on their thrones.

A turtle struts, slow but proud,
While a wandering snail sings out loud.
"Catch me if you can, I'm on a roll!"
It's hard to chase when you're lacking control!

Echoes of the Whispering Trees

Branches sway, speaking low,
Jokes that only they seem to know.
A wise old owl hoots with a grin,
"Who? Me? Never!" with laughter within.

Mice scurry past with a playful squeak,
Dreaming of cheese, they're on a peak.
Their goofy antics, make me giggle,
As they play tag with a delightful wiggle!

In the Shadow of Evergreen Giants

In the woods where squirrels play,
With acorns flying every day.
The trees stretch tall, a leafy crowd,
I swear they laugh, they're just too proud.

A chipmunk trips on a fallen pine,
He shakes his head, calls it a sign.
"These roots are grumpy, old and stout!"
I giggle as he scurries about.

The sun peeks through, a playful tease,
While birds debate about the breeze.
A rabbit's stuck in a hammock made,
He snores like thunder, I'm quite dismayed!

The shadows dance, a wobbly show,
As I chase butterflies to and fro.
In this green realm, where mischief thrives,
Nature's chuckles keep us alive.

Soft Murmurs of Nature's Heart

Beneath the boughs, I hear it clear,
A rustling tune that brings me cheer.
A friendly critter calls my name,
I toss a peanut, it's quite the game!

The bees are buzzing quite a tune,
In rhymes with flowers, a cheeky croon.
They flap their wings, a winged parade,
Pollinating, but never delayed.

A family of ants on a tiny quest,
Carry a crumb—they know the best.
One trips and falls, a crumb's now lost,
His buddies laugh, at no great cost!

With laughter echoing through the trees,
I join the fun, a life of ease.
In whispers soft as downy fluff,
Nature's jokes are just enough!

The Stillness of Pine-Scented Dreams

In dreams of green, I drift and sway,
The fragrance beckons, come and play.
A sleepy bear, upon a log,
Snorts like thunder, gives me a hog!

The pines are gossiping, can't you tell?
Sharing secrets, oh what a spell!
The wind chimes in with a cheeky jest,
Whispering tales of nature's quest.

I spot a fox, with mischief in eyes,
He's up to something, oh what a surprise!
In a game of hide-and-seek he's found,
His sneaky grin—it knows no bounds!

The world spins on, in a leafy dance,
With nature involved, who needs a chance?
In the stillness, beneath the skies,
Wild laughter bubbles—what a surprise!

Underneath the Green Veil

In the glade where shadows peek,
The creatures chatter, all unique.
A wise old tortoise wears a hat,
He's plotting schemes—imagine that!

A family of owls in hilarious plight,
Hooting in sync, just pure delight.
One loses track of time, falls asleep,
While dreams of snacks begin to creep!

The branches sway like happy kids,
Bouncing laughter over the grids.
A crow pops in with a cheeky call,
"Who wants to dance?" he squawks to all!

The sun dips low, a giggly beam,
As shadows blend—a shiny dream.
With nature's jokes, I soak it in,
Under green canopies, life's a win!

Communion with Nature's Majesty

Squirrels chatter, plotting schemes,
Acorns fly, or so it seems.
Beneath the branches, laughter bends,
Nature's jest, where time transcends.

A rabbit hops, thinks it can dance,
With clumsy moves, it takes its chance.
Birds tweet tunes, a croaking band,
Coordinates lost, it's quite unplanned.

Beneath the leaves, the shadows play,
A mossy throne for hide and sway.
The wind whispers jokes in my ear,
A comedy show held right here!

Clouds drift past, taking their time,
Nature's rhythm, a perfect rhyme.
With each giggle, joy expands,
In the forest, laughter stands.

Embraced by the Tallest Friends

The tallest trees, with arms out wide,
Invite the sun to come inside.
Their leafy hair, all wild and free,
Hosts of laughter, just wait and see!

A jaybird leaps from branch to branch,
Thinking it's some kind of dance.
With every flap, a silly scare,
It's gym class for the unaware!

The groundhog grins, a wise old sage,
Peeking out from his leafy cage.
With a grin that never seems to fade,
He gives a chuckle in the glade.

And when the wind begins to sing,
The trees shake hands, like old folks bring.
They toss their stories through the air,
A friendship that's beyond compare.

Golden Moments in Swaying Shadows

Dappled light on grassy floor,
As dancing shadows start to soar.
A bumblebee buzzes, oh so proud,
Mistakenly joins a cotton crowd.

Sunbeams tickle the ferny tongues,
While crickets hum their silly songs.
Grasshoppers try to leap so high,
And plop down flat—oh my, oh my!

As sunshine glimmers through the trees,
A lizard lounges, catching breeze.
With eyes half-shut, he winks with flair,
Says, "Life's too short for full-on care!"

In these moments, joy does bloom,
Nature's laughs dispel the gloom.
With every giggle, breezes play,
In this golden, warm ballet.

A Sanctuary of Scented Air

Fragrant blooms dance with delight,
Breezes chase away the night.
Bees in fancy dress parade,
In this fragrant masquerade.

The pine trees share a hearty laugh,
As squirrels plot their mischief path.
With every rustle, joy reveals,
A comedy fest on leafy wheels.

A plump toad croaks his wisdom out,
"Hop along! There's fun, no doubt!"
As daisies sway, they spill the news,
Of secret picnics and merry blues.

The sun spills golden, sweet perfume,
In this sanctuary, life finds room.
With every chuckle, hopes grow grand,
In nature's joke-filled, green wonderland.

A Solitude Amongst the Needles

In a patch of soft green moss,
A squirrel lost his shiny floss.
He danced and twirled without a care,
As birds above threw jokes to share.

A chubby raccoon joined the fray,
Wearing berries like a bouquet.
They laughed and played a silly game,
While crickets chirped, forgetting shame.

With every tumble, giggles bloomed,
As shadows shifted, brightly groomed.
A party hosted by the trees,
Where nature's laughter drifts with ease.

The needles fell like soft confetti,
While hedgehogs wobbled, never petty.
A solitude, though filled with glee,
In every rustle, they're carefree.

Shade of the Ancient Giants

Beneath the branches, shadows sway,
An owl hoots jokes at end of day.
The trees, they chuckle, bark and nod,
As we dance silly on the sod.

A rabbit tried to hop so high,
But landed in a pie nearby.
With crusty ears and berry stains,
He classifies his life as gains.

A wise old tree with knotted face,
Cracks puns about this woodland place.
While squirrels roll their eyes with glee,
Some acorns laugh, "That's just like me!"

In the shadows, snickers fly,
As chipmunks plan their next supply.
The giants watch, they're in on fun,
Their laughter echoes, never done.

In the Embrace of Pine Boughs

A pine cone hat was all the rage,
Worn by the fox, who took the stage.
He danced a jig, so spry and bright,
While owls rolled eyes and took to flight.

With pine needles as their little drums,
All critters joined, and here it comes!
The rhythm made the branches sway,
As laughter grew, it stole the day.

A family of ants formed a line,
Doing the conga, oh so fine.
While beetles grooved in dapper suits,
In pines and laughter, none dispute.

In the embrace of fragrant boughs,
Where silliness, like breeze, allows.
They share a chuckle, cheer the score,
In every crevice, life's a bore!

The Sigh of the Woodland Whisper

A whisper flutters through the trees,
It tells of mischief, jokes, and fees.
A deer once tripped upon a log,
And landed plop in a muddy bog.

The tale spread fast among the throng,
As rabbits chimed in with a song.
They mimicked her, with floppy ears,
While hedgehogs rolled, dismissing fears.

The whispers laughed with swirling breath,
About the deer's oh-so-funny wreck.
The woods became a stage at night,
With dappled light, a laugh-filled sight.

And under every bough that sways,
Woodland whispers laugh and play.
For nature holds the funniest fables,
As long as we share laughter's tables.

The Nestled Refuge of Aged Wood

In the crook of branches, a squirrel sings,
Gathering acorns, and all sorts of things.
A raccoon rolls by, in a makeshift canoe,
Paddling clumsily, dreaming of stew.

The birds throw a party, they chirp and they screech,
As the wise old owl teaches them how to screech.
He hoots out a joke, and they all fall in fits,
While the mouse on the floor just stares, and he sits.

A deer stops to listen, with one ear in flight,
Thinking, 'Maybe I'll dance if the beat feels just right.'
But instead, he just chuckles, that graceful old beast,
Finding joy among friends is the best kind of feast.

So here in this haven, where laughter's a breeze,
Nature spins stories, never fails to appease.
With every chirp, chortle, and tiny embrace,
Life under aged wood feels like a warm place.

Cradled by Nature's Outstretched Arm

A chipmunk dashes, then takes a quick break,
He spots a big nut, oh, what a great take!
But alas, in a tumble, he trips on a root,
Now he's chasing his snack like a wild, frenzied brute.

A rabbit peeks out, with a wink and a grin,
Says, 'Watch where you hop, it's a gamble, my kin!'
They giggle at folly, while crickets just play,
As shadows stretch long in the fading day.

With mushrooms for stools, the critters convene,
Each one tells a tale, centered on beans.
In this circus of nature, the world feels divine,
With a laugh and a snack, all the creatures align.

So here laughter echoes, in nature's embrace,
A world filled with joy, it's a colossal grace.
Friends gathered together, no worries to harm,
Life thrives in this space, in nature's own arm.

Embracing the Spirit of the Forest

In a tangled green world, a badger lost track,
Now he's wearing a leaf, not a thing that he lacks.
He struts with a grin, like royalty's theme,
While crickets applaud, as they manage to beam.

A goofy old fox, with his wild, sunny flare,
Decides to play tricks, yet he leaps through the air.
He trips on a vine, tumbles, rolls to his feet,
While laughing out loud, he admits it's a feat.

Around the tall trunks, they declare a sweet race,
A snail nearly wins with a slow, patient pace.
While the rest hold their sides, in delightful dismay,
At the hilarity found here, in simple play.

Amidst the tall trees, the spirit ignites,
With giggles and grins, nature winks in the nights.
When wildlife is silly, the heart starts to soar,
Embracing this humor, we long for much more.

Seasons of Strength and Solace

When autumn arrives, the leaves play a joke,
They dance in the wind, on a soft golden cloak.
A bear with a beard made of crisp, crunchy flakes,
Can't help but laugh, as his tummy then aches.

Winter brings snowballs, a fluffy delight,
As friends join the fray in a wild, snowy fight.
A raccoon in a scarf shouts, 'Here's looking at you!'
As a snow-covered squirrel says, 'I'll join in too!'

In spring, tiny flowers begin to all bloom,
With bees buzzing cheerfully, clearing the gloom.
A hedgehog rolls by, wearing one of their hats,
While insects all chuckle, hoping for chats.

Then summer arrives with a warm, lazy sun,
Where critters lounge around, and everyone's fun.
Seasons in laughter, each moment a thrill,
Nature's sweet comedy, always a chill.

Emerald Hues in Quietude

In the forest, a squirrel danced,
A nut in hand, it pranced and pranced.
With acorn cap atop its head,
It twirled around, ambitions fed.

A rabbit laughed, with ears so wide,
Challenged the squirrel, tried to hide.
But tripped on roots, oh what a sight,
The woods erupted in sheer delight.

A turtle watched, so slow and grand,
"Let's race," he said, with calm command.
The race began, but no one cared,
For laughter's prize was highly shared.

So join the fun in leafy lanes,
Where giggles echo, break all chains.
In emerald hues, antics unfold,
In peace and joy, the tales are told.

Forest Whispers at Dusk

A raccoon sneaks with nimble paws,
Raiding picnics, breaking laws.
With crumbs upon his furry face,
He scurries off, quickening his pace.

The owls hoot, a night brigade,
Dressed in shadows, planning charade.
"Who's got the best tree to perch?"
A meeting up, beneath the birch.

The fireflies dance, a sparking crew,
Performing shows for me and you.
But tripping branches lead to falls,
As laughter rings through wooded halls.

So when the dusk begins to creep,
And woodland secrets want to leap,
Join the mischief, let joy cascade,
As the whispers of the night invade.

Tranquility in the Thicket

A beaver builds a dam with glee,
Singing loudly, "Come join me!"
While frogs croak out a ribbit tune,
Quacking softly to the moon.

A sneaky fox with mischief eyes,
In playful chase, it spins and flies.
With every twist, it jumps around,
But trips on roots and tumbles down.

The deer stumble in their run,
Giggling softly, it's all in fun.
With every hop, they snicker bright,
As friends unite in pure delight.

So come embrace the forest's charm,
Where laughter spreads like sunny balm.
In thickets thick, hilarity plays,
In nature's game, we lose our ways.

A Retreat in the Green Shade

In a meadow, a tortoise pretends,
To be fast, but it just amends.
While bunny races, quick and spry,
"Catch me if you can!" it shouts with a sigh.

The butterflies tease, flit and fly,
Creating chaos as they vie.
With each flapping, the tortoise snores,
In leafy dreams, he gently roars.

A singing toad in a mossy choir,
Starts up a song, sparks wild fire.
But frogs forget the words they know,
Creating rhythms with a funny flow.

So gather 'round in leafy space,
Where critters frolic at their pace.
In nature's laugh, let worries fade,
In the green shade, friendships made.

Shadows of the Verdant Keepers

In the forest, whispers giggle,
As squirrels plot their cheeky wiggle.
A chipmunk steals a hiker's snack,
While pondering the next bold attack.

Beneath the leaves, a rabbit pranks,
On unsuspecting adventurer banks.
They hop and dance, quite the display,
In nature's own delightful play.

A fox in shades of orange struts,
With a flair that simply cuts.
He tips his hat, suave and sly,
Inviting us with a mischievous eye.

So sit awhile and take a load,
The forest is a funny road.
Laughter bubbles in rustling trees,
As nature spills its quirky tease.

Serenity in the Sylvan Realm

In the calm where branches sway,
A snail declares it's 'Speedy Day!'
With tiny rounds, he leaves a trail,
While bugs engage in a silly whale.

A parrot perched in laughter's grace,
Cackles loud in a feathered race.
'Watch me fly!' he tries to soar,
But lands with thud—oh, the uproar!

A turtle thinks he's quite the star,
With antics sure to raise the bar.
He trundles forth and takes a bow,
To critters who cannot help but wow.

Laughter echoes through the glade,
Nature's jesters never fade.
In every corner, joy is found,
A sylvan realm where smiles abound.

The Poetry of Pine Needles

A poet sits with pens in hand,
While dancing needles make a band.
They rustle wildly, join the beat,
With verses sprouting from their feet.

A woodpecker proves quite the muse,
Tapping out rhymes, never to lose.
While ants discuss their greatest plight,
Planning parties that last all night.

A beetle dons its tiny hat,
And winks as it chats with the cat.
Sharing stories of the day,
While shadows twist and dance in play.

So gather round, join in the fun,
Our woodland rhyme has just begun.
In every rustle, joke, and hum,
The poetry's alive and young.

Flickering Light Beneath Boughs

In a glade with twinkling sparks,
A raccoon juggles glowing larks.
As fireflies blink without a care,
They light the night with comedic flair.

A chipmunk bops to a silent tune,
Hoping to boogie by the moon.
He takes a spill, but don't you fret,
He rolls right up like a furry pet.

A shadow dances, bold and spry,
While owls hoot their laughter high.
With every flap, the humor flies,
Wings spread wide under starry skies.

So laugh aloud and share the bliss,
In nature's show, it's hard to miss.
A light-hearted charm in every breeze,
Where joy and quirks come with such ease.

Pine Cone Dreams and Whispered Schemes

In the branches, dreams take flight,
Squirrels plotting late at night.
A cone falls down, lands on my hat,
Is it a prank? I think, now that's that!

With every rustle, giggles hide,
Tales of acorns and a slide.
Mice with glasses, reading lore,
What's a pine cone good for? More!

The owls hoot jokes, so wise and sly,
As clouds parade across the sky.
We dance beneath the leafy spree,
In nature's theater, wild and free!

Beneath this dome of green above,
Laughter echoes, friends, and love.
In the pine's embrace, so warm and bright,
With laughter in the soft moonlight.

Nature's Fortress of Solitude

A sturdy fortress, roots dug deep,
Where thoughts can dance and secrets creep.
Pine needles tickle, laughter rolls,
Guarding moments of funny souls.

Lizards dressed in tiny suits,
Debate if bugs are better brutes.
A raccoon thief with nimble paws,
All watchful eyes and chuckled jaws.

The breeze whispers to passing clouds,
Jokes that burst like fluffy shrouds.
Nature's giggle, a soothing balm,
In this wildness, all feels calm.

Underneath, a carpet soft,
Where giggles rise and spirits loft.
In this haven, quirky and bright,
We revel in the sheer delight.

Through the Treetops' Gaze

Up above where the branches sway,
Birds share tales of a silly day.
A feathered friend, in shades of blue,
Tells a joke—the punchline flew!

With squirrels chasing tails in glee,
Every leap, a sight to see.
Pine needles dance on the playful air,
As nature giggles, none can compare.

The sun peeks through, a wink or two,
Lighting up the world, anew.
Where shadows play, and laughter's loud,
We weave our dreams, both young and proud.

In this canopy, life unfolds,
Silly secrets and stories told.
With every rustle and every cheer,
The tree-tops whisper—fun is near!

A Refuge Amidst the Pines

In this realm where whispers dwell,
Mice tell stories, can you tell?
A dandelion crowns a frog,
Telling tales in a piney fog.

An ant parade, all dressed in blues,
Marching forth in little shoes.
Silly antics of their brigade,
Leave behind a polished grade.

Pine trees sway, the wind aligns,
Birds compose their wittiest lines.
We share the shade, our laughter mixed,
In this refuge, we are fixed.

With every glance, a quip, a jest,
Nature's humor, truly the best.
In this spot, let's play and sing,
Among the pines, let joy take wing!

The Gentle Whisper of Green Giants

In the forest, whispers flow,
Trees gossiping, soft and low.
Squirrels chuckle, acorns fly,
Who knew nature's so sly?

Bees buzzing like they're the best,
Chasing flowers, no time to rest.
A rabbit hops, slips on some dew,
Turns to laugh, 'What's a bunny to do?'

Mushrooms giggle, tickled by rain,
Dancing around, but none feel pain.
Leaves rustle, sharing a joke,
'Who's the fool? The one who woke!'

Moonlight peeks through, a curious sight,
Trees pretend to sleep tight at night.
Yet with a wink, they can't resist,
Their funny tales, a twist in the mist.

Tranquil Memories in Leafy Shadows

In the shade, a picnic strewn,
With ants marching like a cartoon.
Sandwiches giggle as bees pass by,
'Hey, save us some!' they can't help but cry.

The old oak winks, woodpecker knocks,
Says, 'Watch out! Here comes the fox!'
Who trips and falls, a clumsy show,
Belly laughs echo, as breezes blow.

Children play, hiding behind,
Each tree a giant, oh so kind.
'Can you see us?' they squeal with glee,
In the leafy shadows, they're all free!

Rolling logs, like slides of fun,
Nature's playground, everyone runs.
Under the boughs, life's a big game,
Where giggles echo, never the same.

Beneath the Tranquil Canopy

Sunshine splatters on the ground,
Making shadows dance around.
A chicken struts, but oh, what clucks!
She's found a worm, hidden in muck.

Lizards lounge, real cool but meek,
In a sunbeam, they hardly speak.
One yawns wide, 'This is the life!'
'Except when my tail gets in a strife!'

The old pine shakes, its needles drop,
Squirrels snicker, 'Time to swap!'
'Your leaves look tired, time to renew!'
As they tumble down, an evergreen crew.

With laughter loud, the day slips by,
As nature winks with a joyful sigh.
Under green arches, the world feels right,
Where even shadows can add delight.

The Calm of Pine-Crowned Heights

Perched high up, a bird takes flight,
Singing songs, oh what a sight!
Wings flap wildly, no care in the world,
While around, the leaves are twirled.

A pinecone drops, a tactical plan,
To land on the heads of a nearby man.
"Ouch!" he exclaimed, looking around,
"Guess it's raining debris, what a sound!"

Down below, a wise old frog,
Dreams of flies while resting on a log.
"Life's no rush, take it slow,"
But then, he leaps, 'Oh no, oh no!'

Up in the treetops, laughter rings,
As critters create their silly flings.
Under branches, in playful heights,
Nature's joy shines, with giggling lights.

A Refuge in Nature's Arms

In the woods where squirrels play,
And birds are having their buffet,
A gnome trips on a hidden root,
Wearing bright red shoes and a suit.

A fox looks on and giggles loud,
As the gnome swirls, feeling so proud,
A tree branch sways, a leaf does flop,
The gnome does a dance, then goes hop.

Sunbeams peek through leaves above,
A puppy joins, he's full of love,
They tumble down a grassy hill,
With laughter ringing, time stands still.

In nature's arms, all worries cease,
Where every creature's found their peace,
The world outside can wait awhile,
In this realm, we've found our style.

Echoes of Roots and Dreams

The old tree stands, so wise and grand,
Its roots curl up like a helping hand,
A rabbit hops with a cheeky grin,
Sipping dew that trickles thin.

Beneath its arms, we tell our tales,
Of silly quests and daring gales,
A beetle joins with a tiny hat,
As everyone laughs, 'What's up with that?'

A toe gets stubbed on a rugged stone,
'That wasn't me!' declares the shone,
A chorus of giggles starts to flow,
As shadows play, and breezes blow.

Underneath this leafy dome,
We find a place that's just like home,
With roots that whisper secrets planted,
And dreams that bounce, a little enchanted.

Lullabies in the Cool Shade

In the cool shade, a songbird sings,
While ants march off with leafy flings,
A cat naps deep, with whiskers spread,
Dreaming of fish dancing in red.

The grasshoppers leap, oh what a sight,
As a turtle thinks, 'Should I join this flight?'
But then he shrugs and munches leaves,
While a squirrel giggles beneath the eaves.

A breeze tickles a dusty old hat,
And the fellow in it grows quite flat,
With a chuckle, he sits tall once more,
Wishing he'd thought to lock the door.

Lullabies hum in nature's key,
Where every critter feels so free,
In this cool, carefree, leafy glade,
Life's tapestry is lovingly laid.

Beneath the Canopy's Comfort

The sunbeams twinkle like little stars,
While a raccoon sneaks off with some jars,
He's planning a feast for the woodland crew,
Served up with a side of wild berry stew.

A turtle sports shades, looking all cool,
As children giggle, Grandpa's the fool,
He slips on a leaf, and with flair he spins,
'Just warming up for the next big wins!'

In the background, a buzzard flies high,
Catching glimpses of mischief nearby,
While under this canopy, chaos reigns,
With laughter echoing in playful chains.

So grab a snack, join the dance,
In the forest, there's always a chance,
To find a friend, to share a laugh,
While nature weaves its carefree path.

Lost in the Green Embrace

In a forest of pretzels, I twirl and roam,
My snack is a twig, a joke for my home.
Squirrels laugh loud as I trip on a root,
Maybe my lunch can disguise as a boot!

Sunlight is giggling, it dances on leaves,
I'm juggling acorns, oh how my heart grieves.
Nature's my playground, but why am I sore?
That squirrel just stole my lunch—what a bore!

The wind starts to whistle, a cheeky little tune,
It rolls through the branches, like a playful cartoon.
I chase after shadows, but they all just flee,
Guess it's just me and this very tall tree!

With laughter around, who cares about lunch?
Underneath the greenery, I'm ready to munch.
A picnic for squirrels, a feast of delight,
Together we'll party into the night!

A Canopy of Serenity

Beneath the green ceiling, a snail winds with cheer,
He's running a race, or so it appears!
The ants on parade wear their hats with such pride,
They march 'round the roots with no secrets to hide.

A breeze tunes the laughter, leaves rustle in glee,
I join in their frolic, just squirrel-sighted me.
The mushrooms all giggle, their caps all aglow,
They fold into fairies, but oh, don't you know?

A rabbit does ballet with grace all around,
And frogs play the drums with a rhythm profound.
I step on a twig and the giggles erupt,
Spinning and laughing, who've I just disrupted?

With joys that are tiny and laughs that are loud,
We dance in our antics, a whimsical crowd.
Each moment a painting, bright colors they share,
In this secret green kingdom, there's fun everywhere!

The Evergreen's Lament

Oh, this tree's got secrets, it whispers, it sighs,
Complains 'bout the squirrels with their twinkling eyes.
"Just one nut per branch! I'm far too refined!"
Yet, branches are tangled in laughs unconfined.

The shadows conspire, they giggle and weave,
A dance for the critters, no time to bereave.
"I'm old and I'm wise," the pine wants to say,
But tripping on roots puts his wisdom at bay.

The birds start a chorus, a quirky refrain,
While the tree rolls its eyes, "Oh, here comes the rain!"
With each raindrop's giggle, it slips and it sways,
Musing on madness that brightens its days.

Yet deep down it knows, through the laughter of life,
That joy's in the jests, amidst all of the strife.
So it sways in the storm, with a grin and a jest,
In nature's dear playground, absurdity's best!

Starlight Filtered Through Needles

As nighttime unfolds with a blanket of stars,
The owls start their gossip, and dance with the cars.
Fireflies are winking, they twirl in delight,
While I try to catch one—oh, what a sight!

A raccoon named Earl is a master of games,
He rolls in the leaves, calling out all our names.
We're chuckling 'til dawn, under moon's tender glow,
With tales of our antics, too wild to bestow.

The pine needles rustle, like secrets they share,
Mysteries of laughter float lightly in air.
The critters all gather, a mischievous crew,
As shadows of giggles dance merrily through.

With the stars as our guides, and the night our friend,
We spin through the forest, this party won't end.
Surrender to whimsy, let joy be the rule,
In this cosmic playground, we're all just a fool!

Dance of the Gnarled Branches

A squirrel in a top hat, he prances about,
Twirling with acorns, he won't leave a doubt.
The branches all giggle, the leaves whisper low,
As twigs form a dance floor, oh, what a show!

The shadows are laughing, the breeze sings a tune,
While worms in the soil cut loose with a swoon.
A raccoon joins in, with moves quite absurd,
He moonwalks right past, while singing a bird.

The gnarled bark chuckles, what a sight to behold,
As pine cones get jiggy, feeling ever so bold.
The sunlight a spotlight, the stage now complete,
In this wacky forest, the fun's hard to beat!

So join in the frolic, don't miss out on the fun,
For when trees throw a party, it can't be outdone.
With laughter and whispers, it's a riotous spree,
In this crazy old world, let the good times be free!

Secrets Shared Among the Trees

In hollows and nooks, the whispers do flow,
Of gossiping bugs who already know.
A worm tells a secret, a tale oh so grand,
While ants start a rumor, they can't quite withstand.

The oak winks at willows, who blush all the more,
"You won't believe what I just heard before!"
The breeze carries laughter, it tickles the leaves,
As branches extend for the latest of thieves.

'Have you seen that chipmunk? He's quite the sly one!"
"His stash is so hefty, I bet he has fun!"
The pine trees all nod, with a rustling sound,
As lush, leafy laughter floats softly around.

And when twilight falls, the secrets won't cease,
The critters keep sharing, with glee never lease.
In shadows they chatter, with jokes and with puns,
A comedy show, lit by a million suns!

The Breath of the Silent Woods

In silence they murmur, with giggles and grins,
The trees lay their bets on who tickles the winds.
A shadow sneezes, oh what a surprise,
The branches shake gently, with raucous replies.

With each rustling whisper, a tale comes alive,
Of critters who plot how to prank and to jive.
The moss holds a secret, lush carpets and green,
As squirrels hold a meeting that's seldom seen.

"There's a hoot owl watching, he's snoozing all day,
While we play our tricks in this silly ballet!"
Laughter erupts, as the laughter grows loud,
The trees, in their wisdom, feel lucky and proud.

Their roots intertwining, they've made a great crew,
Together they chuckle, under skies so blue.
In this wacky silence, where nature's delight,
Even whispers can have a marvelous night!

Twilight Beneath the Evergreens

At twilight the shadows begin to take form,
As hedgehogs come out, they decide to perform.
With dance moves so quirky, they wiggle and sway,
As crickets compose, a delightful ballet.

The evergreens whisper with rustling delight,
Their tips all aglow in the soft fading light.
"A hedgehog's a dancer?" a pine-tree critiques,
"How can he boogie, with all of those spikes?"

The yew shakes his branches, an audience pleaser,
While firs try and twirl, but they fall in a teaser.
"Moss, dust off your boots! Time to strut your stuff!"
The forest erupts, "Oh, this is quite tough!"

So join in the twilight, where laughter thrives bright,
As the forest keeps spinning from day into night.
With chuckles and giggles, they dance in a line,
Making merry and mischief, it's all just divine!

www.ingramcontent.com/pod-product-compliance
Lightning Source LLC
Chambersburg PA
CBHW071853160426
43209CB00003B/538